"The process......ent with established democratic procedure...the federal government has maintained its position from the beginning that the Accord will not be changed...Yet the Canadian public had no part in its formulation."

"Of all subjects, it is Senate reform and the creation of new provinces which will suffer most under the unanimity rule."

"...in respect to future programs...we could end up with a patchwork of programs across the country, which differ in nature and quality."

"...of all Canadians, theirs (the native peoples) might properly be called a "distinct society"...they deserve better consideration than that accorded to them under the Meech Lake Accord."

"Another regrettable possibility would be that...the government of Quebec might believe that to promote its distinct society or identity, it must become a separate state...It is unfortunate that the federal government (and some media) have promoted the idea that rejection of the Meech Lake Accord is a rejection of Quebec."

"The question is: Will Canada become two nations, or worse still, ten?"

"Canadians should not allow themselves to be intimidated by threats, but should ask the question: What will the Meech Lake Accord mean to us and to Canada?"

Marjorie Montgomery Bowker
B.A., LL.B., LL.D.

Published by
Voyageur Publishing
Executive Editor: Sean Fordyce
Cover Concept and Design: Kim Ford and Patrick Fordyce
Production Coordination: George McKenzie of GEMM Graphics

The text was prepared on Apple Computers supplied by
Lasercomp Solutions 109-1220 Old Innes Road, Ottawa.

The publisher received no financial
assistance for this project.

The author has declined all royalties which
have been passed on to the public by way
of a lower sale price for this book

Printed in Canada
Through the services of GEMM Graphics
2022 Kingsgrove Cres. Gloucester, Ontario (613) 748-6613

ISBN: 0-921842-06-6

THE
MEECH LAKE ACCORD

WHAT IT WILL MEAN TO YOU AND TO CANADA

An Independent Analysis

by

MARJORIE MONTGOMERY
BOWKER
B.A., LL.B., LL.D.

Published by
Voyageur Publishing
82 Frontenac Street, Hull, Québec J8X 1Z5
(819) 778-2946

EDITOR'S NOTE

This analysis was first produced in early March 1990 on the author's word processor, then photocopied and distributed at her expense. Copy centres in Ottawa, Edmonton and Vancouver assisted in the distribution.

Bulk orders from book-stores across Canada made it clear that a wider distribution was necessary, and in more durable form.

I approached the author on behalf of Voyageur Publishing and received permission to publish the original manuscript in book form.

This book is unchanged from the original with the following exceptions:

minor typographical corrections;

the addition of the text of the Meech Lake Accord and the proposed Constitutional Amendment; and

an Addendum by the author entitled "What We as Canadians Can Do".

Sean Fordyce
Hull, Quebec
March 28, 1990.

PREFACE

The debate over the Meech Lake Accord has been going on for almost three years. Yet the voices being heard are mainly those of politicians, academics and business people. Rarely do we hear from the average Canadian.

Little wonder, when a recent GALLUP poll, taken in March 1990, showed that 60% of Canadians said they knew little or nothing about the content of the Meech Lake Accord. The Accord is designed to change our Constitution. It is not a lengthy document, but it is complicated, and can only be understood in the light of what has gone before.

There is danger that for want of a better understanding, some Canadians may not care what happens, and leave it to politicians to make the decisions. It is, however, *our* constitution. It is *our* country. It is *our* future.

The purpose of this analysis is simply to present the facts, leaving it to Canadians to formulate their own opinion. It is a personal project, entirely self-financed, and the writer is not accepting revenue from any source, nor any royalties from this book.

Marjorie Montgomery Bowker
B.A., LL.B., LL.D.
Former Judge
Provincial Court of Alberta
Family and Juvenile Divisions
(1966-1983)

Edmonton, Alberta
March 23, 1990

TABLE OF CONTENTS

CHAPTER ONE

CANADA'S PRESENT CONSTITUTION

Canada's basic constitution is an Act of the British Parliament called the *British North America Act of 1867* (now re-named the *Constitution Act 1867*). Though it has undergone amendments over the years, it is still our basic constitutional document. For example, it establishes the House of Commons and Senate, as well as the composition, procedures and powers of each. It sets up the constitutional structure for the provinces. It stipulates the subjects on which Parliament can pass legislation, and those subjects on which the provinces can legislate. It defines the structure of our Courts. This Act (with amendments) remains in force to this day.

Not until 1982 were there major additions to the Canadian constitution. These consisted of two Acts:

1. The *Canada Act 1982* which transferred to the Canadian Parliament the power to amend our constitution -- a power which was formerly vested in the British Parliament. (This is commonly referred to as the "patriation" of our constitution.)

2. The *Constitution Act 1982* which includes the *Canadian Charter of Rights and Freedoms* which for the first time entrenches in our constitution protection of individual rights and freedoms including freedom of religion, assembly, association and the press; as well as a variety of

other rights (legal, democratic, equality, language, mobility).

It is important to note that the *Constitution Act* of 1982, which was initiated by the former Liberal government, was passed by Parliament only after widespread public debate, several inter-provincial conferences, public hearings, and even a constitutional reference to the Supreme Court of Canada. In the end, the Quebec premier, Rene Levesque refused to sign the Act, alleging that French interests were insufficiently protected. However, Quebec members of Parliament, by a large majority, voted in its favour, and it is generally believed that the people of Quebec were in agreement.

The Meech Lake Accord (to be officially called the "Constitutional Amendment 1987") was negotiated by the Conservative government under Prime Minister Brian Mulroney for the stated purpose of settling Quebec's grievances and obtaining its belated signature to the 1982 *Constitution Act*.

Such is the historical background to the Meech Lake Accord.

CHAPTER TWO

HOW THE MEECH LAKE ACCORD CAME ABOUT

The goal of the Meech Lake Accord was a perfectly laudable one -- to obtain Quebec's endorsement to the *Constitution Act* of 1982, from which Quebec had excluded itself.

In May of 1986, the Quebec government under Premier Robert Bourassa presented five demands as conditions for its acceptance of the Constitution. In August of that year, the Premiers' Conference held in Edmonton agreed that priority must be given to getting Quebec back to the bargaining table. It seems that following this, negotiations did get underway amongst senior government officials with a view to addressing Quebec's concerns.

On April 30, 1987 the First Ministers (the Prime Minister and ten provincial premiers) met at Meech Lake (a government retreat north of Ottawa) to deal with Quebec's demands. It was a brief meeting, though reportedly contentious. In the end, the parties produced a "Draft Statement of Principles" which addressed five of Quebec's concerns, plus two additional elements not previously raised by Quebec. This Statement of Principles, which is only three pages in length, was not made public at the time. The premiers agreed to meet again in five weeks to sign the formal legal document which would embody these principles.

Accordingly, on June 3, 1987, the same group of leaders met at the Langevin Building in Ottawa. There they held a secret all-night 11-hour session discussing the document which was to become the Meech Lake Accord. The premiers had been told not to bring their advisors, and those who did were not allowed to have them present, though some of the premiers asked and were allowed to leave the room briefly for consultation. The premiers met in almost total isolation without any opportunity of conferring with cabinet or caucus. In the early morning, Prime Minister Mulroney emerged to say that he and the provincial premiers had rewritten the law "while the nation slept". It is a fact, however, that the public had not seen the wording of the Accord until after the premiers had committed themselves to it. What was presented to the Canadian people was a deal arrived at in secret after an all-night marathon bargaining session. The nation was soon to be told that the Accord must stand as presented without any amendments.

The process which was followed throughout these events is inconsistent with established democratic procedure for amending a nation's constitution. Such a serious step calls for full and open public debate, along with opportunities for discussion and reflection, with preliminary drafts circulated for public scrutiny, before any final document is approved. None of this happened here.

By way of contrast, the B.N.A. Act of 1867 had its ground-work laid three years earlier at the Charlottetown Conference in 1864, followed by two further conferences in London, England and Quebec City. The *Constitution Act* of 1982 was preceded by 18 months of meetings, conferences, new proposals, revisions, compromises and court challenges before its terms were finalized.

There is no precedent for achieving sweeping constitutional change in the manner that was attempted with the Meech Lake Accord.

CHAPTER THREE

EVENTS FOLLOWING THE SIGNING OF THE ACCORD

The federal government made it clear from the beginning that it would not allow any changes or amendments to the Accord as signed at Meech Lake. To become law, it needed to be ratified by Parliament and the ten provincial legislatures.

Its passage through Parliament took the following form: A resolution to approve the Accord was presented to the House of Commons in June 1987. After passing first and second readings, it was referred to a Joint Parliamentary Committee, consisting of 17 members (12 of whom were Conservatives). The Committee held 15 days of hearings during the summer in Ottawa. Eighty witnesses were heard during that short period, and 249 briefs were received, many of which opposed the Accord. It should be noted that even before these hearings began, the Prime Minister, in an exclusive interview with the Canadian Press on June 22, 1987, stated that he would not be influenced by any conclusions of this Committee, nor by opposition or other criticism.

Following the Committee hearings, the resolution easily passed third reading in the Commons because of the large Conservative majority. It was then sent on to the Senate which proceeded to hold hearings of its own across the country, following which it returned the Bill to the Commons with extensive recommended changes. These were rejected, and on June 20, 1988 the Meech

Lake Accord received final ratification by the Parliament of Canada.

As for the provincial legislatures, the Accord was quickly ratified by eight of the ten provinces. However, in respect to two provinces, there was a change in government before the Accord was approved.

In New Brunswick in October 1987, a Liberal government under Premier Frank McKenna, won all seats in the provincial legislature replacing the former Conservative government under Premier Hatfield (who had signed the Accord). In Manitoba, in April 1988, the N.D.P. government under Howard Pawley (who also had signed the Accord) was replaced by a minority Conservative government. The Liberal Leader, Sharon Carstairs, made it clear from the outset that any attempt to ratify the Accord would result in the downfall of the government. Neither of these provinces -- New Brunswick or Manitoba -- has signed the Accord as of this date (March 1990).

The Newfoundland legislature under Premier Peckford was one of the first to ratify the Accord. However, his government has since been replaced by the Liberals under Premier Clyde Wells, who has become one of the most vocal opponents to the Accord and threatens to revoke his province's ratification. For a brief time during January 1990, British Columbia Premier Vander Zalm indicated that he too might be withdrawing his support for the Accord unless changes were made. He has since modified his stand.

Very few provinces held any public hearings before ratifying the Accord. However Manitoba and New Brunswick, which have withheld ratification, each held public hearings, following which they have confirmed their position that they cannot support the Accord without amendments.

As for my own province of Alberta, the Conservative government under Premier Don Getty (one of the most vigorous supporters of the Accord) declined to hold public hearings. The N.D.P. Official Opposition, however, did hold hearings throughout the province in September 1987. A total of 106 oral submissions were made (including one from this writer) plus 25 additional written submissions. The Report dated November 3, 1987, stated that "not one of those who presented briefs were in favour of the Accord as it stood". Based on these results, the Opposition presented to the Alberta legislature ten well-reasoned suggestions for amendment. However, the Alberta legislature on December 7, 1987 approved the Accord as it stood, which was no surprise given the substantial Conservative majority.

The most serious deficiency is that no national public debate was ever held. This is regrettable because the average citizen cannot be expected to understand the complex implications of a constitutional document such as the Meech Lake Accord without the benefit of informed national debate. We are not talking here about minor legislative amendments, but rather about sweeping constitutional and political changes which will re-shape our nation for generations to come.

CHAPTER FOUR

WHAT IT SAYS

The Meech Lake Accord is not a lengthy document -- just under a dozen pages in all -- but it is overlaid with references and cross-references, making understanding difficult. Parts of it are poorly drafted, like a patchwork of constitutional amendments. If ratified, it would be called the "Constitution Amendment 1987" and would be added to Canada's constitutional Acts described in Chapter One above.

The purpose of the Accord, as already stated, was to deal with Quebec's grievances arising from the *Constitution Act 1982,* which Premier Levesque had refused to sign. His successor, Premier Robert Bourassa in 1986 presented five demands to be met before he would sign the Constitution. These original five demands were:

1. recognition of Quebec as a distinct society;

2. a provincial role in appointments to the Supreme Court;

3. a greater provincial role in immigration;

4. limits on federal power in federal-provincial shared-cost programs;

5. a veto for Quebec on constitutional amendments.

The Meech Lake Accord deals with all five of Quebec's demands and gives effect to them all. Some provisions are said to have even exceeded Quebec's expectations. Granting such special privileges to Quebec would give it a status not enjoyed by any of the other provinces. Yet the endorsement of all premiers at Meech Lake was essential. In order to obtain approval of the other nine premiers to the Quebec arrangement, the Prime Minister agreed to give similar wide powers to all of the provinces. Not surprisingly, the prospect of such vastly increased provincial powers might well have proved irresistible to the premiers. This may partly explain how consensus was so readily achieved for the Meech Lake Accord. The question is, however -- at what cost to Canada?

What the Meech Lake Accord has done is to transfer to all provinces powers which properly belong to the central government, if Canada is to remain a cohesive unified nation. Just as some issues are best resolved at municipal or provincial levels, others are clearly best left to a government that speaks for all Canadians.

Instead of a strong federal system such as we have enjoyed for over a century, Canada could become fragmented into something resembling ten fiefdoms, each headed by its own miniature prime minister. Yet Canada needs a strong national government to speak and act for all Canadians, to be the centre of gravity, to resolve regional disparities and to respond to national crises.

Canadians who wish to retain a strong Canada see the flaws in the Meech Lake arrangement, and possible disastrous consequences for our nation.

Even beyond the five Quebec demands, the Meech Lake Accord includes two additional provisions relating to all provinces:

1. the right of provincial governments to make nominations for the Senate;

2. the entrenchment of annual "First Ministers' Conferences" to initiate future constitutional change.

Perhaps the most troubling provision in the Meech Lake Accord is the granting of a veto to each province and to the federal government concerning significant constitutional amendments in the future - including Senate Reform and the creation of new provinces. Under our present law (*Constitution Act 1982*), such amendments require the consent of only seven provinces (plus the federal government), provided those provinces represent 50% of the total Canadian population. The Meech Lake Accord with its unanimity rule will make future constitutional changes of this nature very difficult.

For proponents of Senate reform, there is little likelihood of achieving unanimity amongst all the provinces on such a contentious issue. One wonders why Alberta's Premier Don Getty (for example) so readily signed the Accord, knowing that his long-cherished hope of a Triple-E Senate could be defeated by a single vote.

To summarize the effect of the Meech Lake Accord, there are these overall considerations: special status for Quebec could weaken our nation. Special powers to all ten provinces could weaken our nation ten-fold. The question is: Will Canada become two nations, or worse still, ten?

On the following pages is a detailed analysis of what the Meech Lake Accord provides.

CHAPTER FIVE

IMMIGRATION

There has been a sharing of power over immigration, as between the federal and provincial governments, ever since the B.N.A. Act of 1867 (section 95). In case of conflict, federal law prevails.

Immigration is covered in two segments of the Meech Lake Accord: first, in the Accord itself (section 95A-E), and second, in an Agreement which is incorporated in, and which accompanies the Accord.

WHAT THE MEECH LAKE ACCORD DOES

In respect to Quebec

What the Meech Lake Accord does is to write into the Constitution an agreement (called *Cullen-Couture*) which was entered into between Ottawa and Quebec in 1978. That agreement gave to Quebec a role in selecting immigrants for its province. The Meech Lake Accord goes further -- guaranteeing that Quebec will receive a fixed share of all immigrants entering Canada each year. This share will be equal to Quebec's proportion of the Canadian population (at present this is approximately 25%) -- to which may be added a further 5% at the option of Quebec.

The Accord further provides that the federal government will no longer be involved in providing integration services (language and culture) for immigrants entering Quebec. The Quebec government will handle these services and will receive "reasonable compensation" for doing so.

In all fairness, no one would object to Quebec having a role in the selection of its immigrants, and being entitled to a proportionate share of Canadian immigrants, especially in the light of Quebec's concern about declining birth rates. However, the transfer of integration services (which means the orientation of immigrants to their new life in Canada) is a serious abandonment by the federal government of a national responsibility. There could be a risk of the integration process focusing more on Quebec than on Canada.

In respect to the other provinces

The Meech Lake Accord would allow other provinces to "negotiate" with the federal government for immigration agreements "appropriate" to their "needs and circumstances" (section 95A). Quebec would have some advantage, however, in having an arrangement already in place, and on terms which might be broader than those which other provinces are likely to negotiate. For example, any new agreement must not be "repugnant" to "national standards and objectives" enacted by Parliament [section 95 B (2)]. This restriction would not have applied to Quebec.

In respect to the federal government

It will continue to have control over the classes of immigrants and the level of immigration.

THE EFFECT OF
THE MEECH LAKE ACCORD ON IMMIGRATION

Assuming that agreements are concluded with some or all of the remaining nine provinces, we could end up with ten immigration policies instead of one. In the end, provinces could be competing for immigrants, or for a special class of immigrants. Some, for example, might prefer only well-to-do immigrants, and be less willing to accept Asian and Latin-American refugees.

As for the immigrants themselves, if provincial quotas were in effect, immigrants could be deprived of freedom to settle in the province of their choice. They might even have to shop around for the easiest province to enter.

However, the most serious feature of the Accord is allowing language and cultural integration services to be provided at the provincial level, instead of by the federal government, as has always been the policy. Immigrants enter Canada to become Canadian citizens, and to develop a sense of attachment to Canada, not to become culturally and linguistically identified with a particular province.

Infinitely better is a single national immigration policy (as at present) with Quebec (because of its particular nature) being accorded a special status within that policy. That special status could well include control over selection, and a guaranteed quota of immigrants. Transfer of integration services is, however, very questionable.

SUMMARY

The Meech Lake immigration provision could add to the confusion already existing in Canada's immigration system. It will create a fragmentation of services for immigrants. It represents an ill-advised capitulation to the provinces of a power which is national in scope and which is properly a federal responsibility.

CHAPTER SIX

NOMINATIONS TO THE SUPREME COURT OF CANADA

Since the 1949 abolition of Canadian appeals to the Privy Council in Britain, the Supreme Court of Canada has been our final court of appeal. It is the last resort for Canadian litigants and for interpretations of the constitution. It is properly referred to as "the pinnacle of our legal system".

A high degree of legal competence is required of its members as well as high moral character, talent, experience and commitment.

PRESENT PROCEDURE
FOR APPOINTMENT OF JUDGES

Judges of the Supreme Court have been appointed by the federal cabinet ever since the Court was established in 1875. There are nine judges, including a Chief Justice, with Quebec having three permanent seats. The three Quebec seats assure the presence on the Court of judges knowledgeable of the Quebec Civil Code in relation to appeals from Quebec. The mandatory retirement age for judges is 75. The present Court has six men and three women judges.

Though there is no fixed rule, the general policy (apart from the three Quebec judges) is that out of the remaining six, three will come from Ontario, two from the four western provinces, and one from Atlantic Canada. This distribution conforms to population ratios.

The actual appointment is made by the federal cabinet on the recommendation of the Minister of Justice. The Minister usually consults with the Bar in the region from which the appointment is made, but there is no input from provincial governments as such. At the Supreme Court level, political considerations are at a minimum. In recent years, many appointments have been of judges already serving in superior courts in the provinces, especially those with experience in courts of appeal. There has been an effort by governments to appoint the best persons for positions on Canada's highest court, and this has been true under the Mulroney government as well.

WHAT THE MEECH LAKE ACCORD WILL DO

The Meech Lake Accord will make the following changes in the appointment of judges:

1. When a vacancy occurs amongst the three Quebec judges, the federal cabinet (Governor-General-in-Council) will appoint a person whose name has been submitted by the government of Quebec. This means that Quebec's nominee will automatically be appointed with no federal input into the selection. Quebec will not be competing with any other part of Canada in submitting its nominee. In other words, it has unqualified control over the naming of its three judges.

2. When a vacancy occurs amongst the other six judges, all the remaining nine provinces can submit names. The federal government will appoint a judge from the names submitted, provided that person is "acceptable to the Privy Council of Canada" (which is the federal

cabinet). This means, in effect, that the remaining nine provinces will be competing to have their nominee accepted. There is nothing to prevent a single province submitting several names. Then from all the names submitted, the final selection must be "approved" by Ottawa -- which is not so with the Quebec appointees.

Thus Quebec is placed in a favoured position in regard to Supreme Court of Canada appointments. But all the other provinces are given a comparable (though not equivalent) role -- one that has, until now, been the sole prerogative of the federal government.

SOME PREVIOUS PROPOSALS FOR APPOINTMENT OF JUDGES

Various proposals have been made over the years as to how Supreme Court judges should be appointed. Suggestions extend back over some 20 years and have included the following proposals:

- consulting with the Canadian Bar Association;

-appointment of a special advisor on judicial appointments;

-conferring with provincial attorneys-general; and

-more recently, a report by the Canadian Bar Association in 1985 entitled "The Appointment of Judges in Canada". After stating that judicial appointments should be based on merit and excellence alone, this Report recommended that the appointing power remain with the federal government. Appointments would be made in consultation with provincial attorneys-general and an advisory committee of lawyers and judges.

As a result of the latter report, for courts other than the Supreme Court of Canada, committees were set up in various provinces with power to designate as "qualified" or "not qualified" persons whose names have been submitted by the federal government.

Thus for over 20 years, Canada has been experimenting with various systems for appointing judges. None has been entirely satisfactory.

There is no precedent for the appointment procedure prescribed in the Meech Lake Accord. Once implemented, whether good or bad, it would become entrenched in our constitution.

NEED FOR IMPARTIALITY

The prime consideration in the appointment of judges is to ensure their impartiality. Judicial independence requires that judges have no association or interest beyond the matters before the court which would have an influence on their judgment.

In particular, cases involving interpretation of the *Charter of Rights and Freedoms,* which are increasing in volume, require the Court to perform a quasi-political role as never before. This will make it increasingly important that judges be immune from political influence arising from their appointment. It is not unnatural to assume that most provincial governments would choose nominees who are known to be sympathetic to the provincial position on constitutional or other issues. One such controversial issue that could arise, and on which certain provinces have entrenched positions, is that concerning aboriginal rights. It could be important to some provinces to have a nominee who reflected the provincial view, yet the national interest could be compromised.

Canadians may wish to ponder whether judicial appointments under the Meech Lake Accord will assure the necessary degree of detachment for the judges of Canada's highest court.

PROVINCIAL GOVERNMENT NOMINEES

Until now, provincial governments have not been parties to the selection of judges for the superior courts or Courts of Appeal in the provinces, or for the Supreme Court of Canada. However Provincial Courts, whose judges outnumber all other categories, are the sole responsibility of the provincial governments, including the appointment of judges.

The practice in most countries is that judges of their highest court are appointed by the national government. Australia in 1979 modified this practice slightly by requiring the federal government to consult with the states in appointments to the High Court. West Germany allows the states to take part in selection of judges for the federal appellate courts. However, the kind of role which the Meech Lake Accord allots to the provinces has no parallel in any other federal system.

EFFECT OF THE MEECH LAKE ACCORD ON THE SUPREME COURT

The present system in Canada whereby the federal government alone appoints judges is most likely to assure an over-all balance amongst the judges in respect to race, gender and geographic region. It is also the system most likely to preserve collegiality on the bench, which is essential to the court's proper functioning. With all nine provinces submitting nominations for the six non-Quebec seats, there is no assurance that the regional composition of the court will be maintained. There is nothing in the Accord to prevent some future federal government from appointing judges from one region alone, rather than on the basis of regional distribution, which now prevails.

Over the past decade, excellent appointments have been made of judges who are already experienced in lower courts. Not all provincial cabinets would be aware of suitable nominations across Canada in this category. Such names might never appear on provincial government nomination lists. The Court would thus be deprived of the added strength which such appointments would provide.

WEAKNESSES IN THE MEECH LAKE ACCORD

1. If the federal government is unwilling to approve any of the provincial nominees, there is no mechanism in the Accord for settling the impasse other than leaving the seat vacant.

2. The Accord does not make it clear how many nominations an individual province may submit -- be it one, or several, or a list.

3. Because of provincial competition for the six non-Quebec seats, no single province can have strong expectations that its nominee will receive the appointment. As a result, there could be a high level frustration with the system on the part of provincial governments.

4. Provincial nominees are likely to reflect the political slant of the government which nominated them. Yet the Supreme Court must assure that national interests are paramount.

5. The Northwest Territories and the Yukon do not share in the nominating power, since they are not yet "provinces". Yet their combined population

is 75,000, and they are achieving considerable autonomy in other fields.

CONCLUSION

There was no need for the federal government to make concessions to the provinces to the extent it has done in the Meech Lake Accord respecting appointments to the Supreme Court.

The Accord far exceeds the demands which Quebec made as a condition for signing the 1982 Constitution. Quebec asked for the right to "participate in" and "consent to" judicial appointments. This demand could have been met by establishing a selection committee consisting of lawyers and judges and representatives of the provincial and federal governments. Instead of that, the Accord has decentralized the appointment procedure and politicized the process.

The effect of the Meech Lake Accord is to entrench in the Constitution for years to come a procedure that has been neither tested nor proven. Where changes to our constitution are made, Canadians have a right to expect the best system possible by way of replacement. The question is: Does the Meech Lake proposal assure this?

CHAPTER SEVEN

NOMINATIONS TO THE SENATE

The Senate was created in Canada's original constitution, the B.N.A. Act of 1867. It now has 104 members, with seats distributed as follows:

Quebec 24
Ontario 24
Maritime Provinces 24
    (10 for Nova Scotia; 10 for New
       Brunswick; 4 for P.E.I.);
Western provinces 24
    (6 each for Manitoba, Saskatchewan,
       Alberta and British Columbia);
Newfoundland 6
Yukon and Northwest Territories, one each.

Senators have always been appointed solely by the federal cabinet. Mandatory retirement is at age 75. All bills passed by the elected House of Commons are sent on to the Senate for approval before becoming law. In most cases, the Senate approves the bills; sometimes it holds public hearings before approving; it may recommend changes, in which case the bill goes back to the Commons for another vote. The Senate's legislative powers are much the same as those of the House of Commons, except that the Senate cannot initiate money bills. The Senate serves as a kind of final "watch-dog" on legislation, assuring that all interests have been considered. It has acted in this capacity for 120 years.

In recent times there have been pressures to reform the Senate to give the regions a stronger voice in Ottawa. Much of the agitation for change has come from western provinces which feel they are insufficiently represented.

It is important to note that Senate reform was not included in Quebec's original demands. Its inclusion in the Accord was largely at the insistence of the western premiers.

Not everyone agrees on the need for Senate reform. There are those who wish no reform at all; others who are opposed to the Senate's very existence and for that reason will not discuss its possible reform. Though the media and others frequently berate the Senate as a sanctuary for political patronage, a government poll (Decima) in August 1989 found that the average Canadian thinks well of the Senate and of Senators, indicating that there is a body of opinion which is comfortable with the Senate as it is.

WHAT THE MEECH LAKE ACCORD DOES AND WHAT IT FAILS TO DO

Under the Meech Lake Accord, the federal government would retain the right to appoint Senators. But it would have to make its choice from among "names" submitted by the government of the province where the vacancy occurs. The person chosen must be "acceptable" to the federal government.

The effect of this amendment is to change the procedure for appointment of Senators. Nominees from the provinces are likely to be political favourites (even more so than with nominees to the Supreme Court), creating a kind of political patronage at the provincial level. However, the implications here would not be as serious as with judicial nominees.

It is not so much what the Meech Lake Accord does in regard to the Senate as what it *fails* to do. While changing the method of appointment, it still leaves unchanged such crucial Senate issues as defining its role, function and powers, and assuring that its members are equitably distributed. Changes such as these could be achieved more easily under the present amending formula than would be possible under the Meech Lake Accord which will require unanimous agreement among all the provinces.

Canadians are being told that unless the Meech Lake Accord is approved, Senate reform will be impossible. The truth is that reform will be infinitely more difficult if it *is* approved because of the unanimity rule which will govern future changes.

The advocates of Senate reform should not have allowed themselves to be deluded into signing the Accord without insisting at least on entrenchment of some basic principle of Senate reform, whether it be the so-called "Triple-E Senate", or some other concept. All they got was the promise of annual conferences with Senate reform "on the agenda". This does not really mean much. To be "included on the agenda" does not ensure that discussion will necessarily follow, certainly not that agreement will be reached. Being included on the agenda could continue indefinitely, without ever producing results.

THE TRIPLE-E SENATE

This is a concept developed by Alberta Premier Don Getty and approved in principle at a conference of western premiers. The words mean that the reformed Senate must be "elected, equal and effective". Senators would be elected -- presumably with an *equal* number from each province. As to the word "effective", no one has really defined that term. One wonders what further powers are contemplated to make the Senate "effective" beyond those which it already enjoys. As mentioned earlier, its powers are almost equivalent to those of the House of Commons. If two elected bodies -- the Senate and the House of Commons -- are to exist side by side with roughly parallel powers, it will require a great deal of negotiating to define their separate roles. Even more fundamental than this, however, it could upset our system of "responsible government" under which the cabinet is chosen from the majority party in government. We could be moving in the direction of the American system, which is seen by many as less effective.

THE ALBERTA
SENATE ELECTION - OCTOBER 1989

Since ratifying the Accord, the Alberta government proceeded in October 1989 to hold an election to fill the one Alberta Senate vacancy, even though there is no constitutional basis to permit such an election. Even if the Meech Lake Accord had been passed (which it had not), there is no provision, even in the Accord, for *electing* a Senator. Several candidates, representing various political parties and independents entered the race. The successful candidate was a member of one of the province's opposing parties. His name was submitted to the Prime Minister, who declined to make the appointment, saying (quite properly) that even under the Meech Lake Accord, the government is to be furnished with a list of names from which it will appoint a person acceptable to it, not simply a single name.

The apparent purpose of this election was to promote Senate reform. However there is no legal basis anywhere for electing a Senator, with or without the Meech Lake Accord. Simply to elect someone to an unreformed Senate accomplishes nothing; nor does it address the chief complaint, which is regional inequalities. At best, it is a piecemeal attempt at reform and it has no constitutional validity. As at the time of writing (March 1990) Alberta's elected Senator had not received the hoped-for appointment to the Senate.

CONCLUSION

What the Meech Lake Accord failed to do was to include any commitment by the premiers to principles of Senate reform. The folly is that the premiers most bent on Senate reform should have settled for so little in signing the Accord in its present form. It leaves almost no hope, under the Meech Lake unanimity rule, of ever achieving the sweeping reforms they seek.

Quebec Premier Robert Bourassa has since made it clear that there will be no discussion of Senate reform until the Accord becomes law. The opportunity for addressing this issue may thus have been lost at Meech Lake, and may never emerge again.

CHAPTER EIGHT

THE UNANIMITY RULE: THE AMENDING FORMULA

This is a further comment on the rule discussed in the previous chapter on Senate Reform.

Every constitution includes a procedure by which it can be amended. As previously explained (chapter four), the law up to now, in regard to major amendments, has been reasonable -- requiring approval by the federal government and by seven provinces representing 50% of Canada's population.

The Meech Lake Accord significantly broadens the number of subjects requiring unanimous approval, and effectively gives a veto power to all the provinces (in addition to that of the federal government) over important amendments. In a very real sense, the Meech Lake Accord will "encase our constitution in stone", creating great difficulties in making significant changes in future, especially in regard to Canada's national institutions.

This is why Canadians must be very sure that the Meech Lake Accord is what they want, as it is not likely to be easily changed.

Although Quebec asked for a veto on constitutional amendments, that demand could have been met by giving to Quebecers a veto over constitutional amendments which specifically affect them. But to have given all provinces a general right of veto effectively freezes hope for significant constitutional development in the future.

The unanimity rule will apply not only to Senate reform (as explained in the previous chapter), but it will apply as well to such matters as proportional representation for the provinces in the House of Commons; the Supreme Court of Canada; and the establishment of new provinces. All of these matters under present law (*Constitution Act 1982*) require approval of only seven provinces -- not ten, as under the Accord.

Of all subjects, it is Senate reform and the creation of new provinces which will suffer most under the unanimity rule.

CHAPTER NINE

THE CONCERNS OF NORTHERN CANADIANS: THE YUKON AND NORTHWEST TERRITORIES

These two territories have a combined population of 75,000 people (the Northwest Territories with 52,000 of whom 58% are natives; the Yukon with 23,000, 25% being native). The Northwest Territories is the largest political subdivision in Canada, comprising 33% of our nation's total area. Most of Canada's aboriginal peoples live in these territories.

Because they are "territories" and not "provinces", they are still subject to administration from Ottawa, though over the past decade they have been gradually progressing towards provincial status. Their Executive Councils formerly appointed by Ottawa are now elected, as are the Territorial Assemblies, with a Commissioner in each, being the only federally-appointed official. Progress is also being made with the federal government toward settlement of native land claims, and in 1988 the Northwest Territories reached an agreement in principle with Ottawa for increased control over energy resources. It is not surprising then, that there has been a growing movement among Northerners to become designated as provinces within Canada.

However, the Meech Lake Accord will make that very difficult. It will require a constitutional amendment with the unanimous consent of all ten legislatures and Parliament, any one of which could veto any such proposal. The motivation for exercising such a veto would be the hope of a province laying claim to some of the land area, or more likely to the mineral resources.

In the past, when other provinces were created (such as Alberta, Saskatchewan or Newfoundland) this was done simply by negotiating an Agreement with Ottawa. However, with the provinces becoming part of the process (as they will under Meech Lake), any one province could block the establishment of a new province or provinces in Canada's north.

Creating this barrier to admission of new provinces -- as the Meech Lake Accord has done -- is a slight to Northern Canada, and to the aboriginals and others who live there.

The following complaints have been voiced by the Territories concerning the Meech Lake Accord:

1. Despite their geographical area, and having the largest native population in Canada, they had no part in the secret negotiations leading up to the Meech Lake Accord in 1987.

2. Because they are not provinces, they will have no right to nominate persons for the Senate.

3. They will not be permitted to furnish nominees for judges of the Supreme Court of Canada.

4. They will have no representative at the annual "Conferences of First Ministers" when Senate reform will be on the agenda.

5. They will have no veto over future constitutional amendments, such as that enjoyed by the provinces.

6. They will have little hope of becoming provinces for the reasons stated above.

As a matter of interest, the Yukon Territorial government in 1988 brought a court action seeking a declaration that (*inter alia*) the Prime Minister breached a duty of fairness in failing to invite Yukon representatives to attend the Meech Lake meeting or to consult with them before agreeing to any Constitutional Amendment. However, the Court of Appeal of the Yukon Territory held ([1988] 2 W.W.R. 481) that courts of law do not have jurisdiction over the process of legislation.

Suffice to say, the Yukon and Northwest Territories are unique in Canada as being the home of most of Canada's native Indians, Metis and lnuit, many with a history which predates European colonization. Of all Canadians, theirs might properly be called a "distinct society". In any case, they deserve better consideration than that granted to them under the Meech Lake Accord.

CHAPTER TEN

ENTRENCHMENT OF ANNUAL FIRST MINISTERS' CONFERENCES

The Meech Lake Accord provides for constitutional conferences to be held at least once a year, attended by the ten premiers and the Prime Minister. This was not among Quebec's demands.

The agenda for these meetings must include Senate reform and fisheries, and "such other matters as are agreed upon". These latter words suggest that no other matter will be added unless the premiers agree. Does this mean that subjects such as aboriginal rights, language or multiculturalism (as examples) might never be included because some premier objects?

"Senate reform" was included at the insistence of Alberta's Premier Don Getty, and "fisheries" was included at the insistence of the Atlantic provinces -- presumably as a condition for their signing the Accord. These items will remain on the agenda for years, possibly forever, as there is no provision for their removal. To require an item to be "included on the agenda" (as the Meech Lake Accord does) is really meaningless. It does not ensure either a meaningful discussion or action. The fact that conferences are convened annually removes any urgency to take any definitive action on these issues.

As to what else the premiers do at these conferences is not clear. Because they are called "constitutional conferences" presumably they will be discussing constitutional amendments.

If this means that the premiers can initiate constitutional changes by meeting annually behind closed doors (as was done at Meech Lake), the procedure (to say the least) is questionable. Are they likely to make commitments (as they did at Meech Lake) without earlier consulting with their cabinets or legislatures, and (more importantly) the public? If so, it would represent a serious erosion of the democratic system.

Thus, these conferences could be either very sterile -- by discussing Senate reform and fisheries *ad infinitum* --- or they could become very threatening to the country if they serve to concentrate in the hands of 11 individuals (who happen to be the premiers of the day) control over constitutional amendments without legislative or public consultation. The potential risk here could make this one of the most dangerous provisions in the Meech Lake Accord.

CHAPTER ELEVEN

FEDERAL SPENDING POWERS: SHARED-COST PROGRAMS

CHANGES UNDER THE MEECH LAKE ACCORD

Under the Meech Lake Accord, a province can choose not to participate in national shared-cost programs which may be established in future by the federal government in fields of exclusive provincial jurisdiction. Instead, a province will be permitted to carry on a "program or initiative" of its own, provided it is "compatible with national objectives", and receive "reasonable compensation" if it does so.

The federal government has for many years been prepared to spend money on services which are not normally a federal responsibility. The reason the federal government has been sharing the cost of such programs is to equalize access by all Canadians to the same level of services, regardless of the province in which they live. The provinces must agree to "cost-share" these programs and to administer them within their jurisdiction. Examples of existing shared-cost programs are health care, post-secondary education and social welfare, under the Canada Assistance Plan which has been operating for over 20 years.

A justification for the present system is that the federal government with general authority over taxation, uses the shared-cost programs as a means of distributing wealth from taxation with a view to attaining greater social justice for all citizens.

Some critics say these programs are an interference with provincial powers. They base their argument on the fact that to qualify for funding, provinces must comply with conditions set out by the federal government. Quebec has long been concerned that in accepting federal funds, it may lose control over policy and program management. It was for this reason that Quebec made an arrangement with the federal government some years ago to opt-out of the Canada Pension Plan and to establish the Quebec Pension Plan in its place.

WHAT THE ACCORD SAYS

It will be useful to examine just what the Meech Lake Accord says about future shared-cost programs (section 106A). The following is a summary:

- the changes apply only to new programs established after the Accord comes into force. It has no bearing on programs already operating;

- it relates only to "national" programs, those which apply to all of Canada, not just to a region;

- it allows a province to choose not to participate. Whether this means they must opt-out when the program is being set up, or if they can withdraw later, is not clear;

- if a province does opt-out, and if it carries on a "program or initiative" which is "compatible with national objectives", it will be entitled to "reasonable compensation". What is meant by "initiative" is not clear. Usually it means an urge to do something, not necessarily doing it. Nor is it clear who determines "national objectives". The word "objectives" is vague and abstract. "National standards" would be a more precise requirement;

- the term "reasonable compensation" is equally vague. How will it be assessed and by whom?

This section is replete with ambiguities. It is sometimes said "let the courts decide". However, it is not a proper burden to be thrust on the courts -- asking them to do what the drafters of legislation have failed to do.

Quite apart from these drafting flaws, the Article speaks of the "Government of Canada" establishing programs, and the "government of a province" opting out. Shared-cost programs are usually established not by cabinet order but by Act of Parliament. Likewise, decisions on "opting out" and devising substitute programs would normally be a subject for the provincial legislature. The effect here, as in other parts of the Accord, is to concentrate power in the Executive rather than in the Legislative branch of government.

HOW IT WILL AFFECT
FUTURE SHARED-COST PROGRAMS

Section 106A was obviously meant to limit the ability of the federal government to attach conditions on the spending of its funds by the provinces. Yet if the federal government is to disburse large sums of money in this fashion, it would seem a matter of fiscal responsibility to set uniform standards and conditions for their use. Only thus can the federal government be assured that all provinces benefit on an equal basis as a result of any particular program.

There could be a number of results from the changed policy under the Accord. If there is the likelihood of provinces choosing not to participate, Ottawa might abandon national shared-cost programs altogether, which could be a great loss to average Canadians. Instead, Ottawa might establish regional programs in place of national ones. The system would then become competitive, with no assurance of equal benefits to the various regions. The federal government might even replace national programs by direct grants to individuals or institutions, where there would be less need to consult the provinces. Any one of these alternatives would represent a loss of equitable benefits for Canadians.

It is unlikely, in view of current fiscal restraints, that any new major cost-shared programs will be established by the federal government in the near future. However, no one knows what will be the needs or expectations of Canadians in, say, 10, 20 or 50 years. There are a number of possible programs which might have to be considered in the future, and which might lose their national character because of the opting-out clause in the Meech Lake Accord. Some possible programs are these: an Environmental Protection Program, a National Dental Plan, a National Auto Insurance Program, a Disability Insurance Plan, a National Day-Care Program, a National Legal Aid Plan, a National Tourism Program.

To be effective, such programs would have to operate nation-wide with costs shared between federal and provincial governments. Because of the Meech Lake Accord, and the possibility of provinces not choosing to participate, programs of this kind might never become established on a national basis.

POSSIBLE EFFECT OF THE FREE TRADE
AGREEMENT ON NATIONAL PROGRAMS

We need to be aware of an Article in the *Canada-U.S. Free Trade Agreement* which has a bearing on what Canada can do in future by way of national programs. It is Article 2010 entitled "Monopolies". That term is meant to refer to any plan, scheme or system for providing a national service, which Americans view as a monopoly. If Canada were to introduce any new national program such as those described above, Article 2010 would require us to give advance notice to the United States, engage in consultation if they so requested, and then be prepared to compensate American private interests which might suffer reduced business profits when these services become available through government, rather than by private companies.

The Meech Lake Accord, combined with the Free Trade Agreement, could be a double blow to future national programs in Canada.

LONGER-TERM IMPLICATIONS

National shared-cost programs have been a unifying force within our country. People can move about from province to province and find the same services available. Under the Accord, in respect to future programs, if provinces choose not to participate, we could end up with a patchwork of programs across the country, which differ in nature and quality. An important uniting link would be broken.

CHAPTER TWELVE

THE "DISTINCT SOCIETY" CLAUSE

We come now to the most controversial
provision in the Meech Lake Accord -- the recognition
that Quebec constitutes within Canada a distinct society.
The Constitution of Canada must be interpreted in a
manner consistent with that fact. The government and
legislature of Quebec must "preserve and promote" the
"distinct identity" of Quebec.

Quebec even now is a distinct society in the sense
that it already enjoys special rights in earlier
Constitutions. The B.N.A. Act of 1867 recognizes
Quebec civil law (section 94) as distinct from the English
common law; French is recognized as an official
language (section 133). The 1982 Constitution (from
which Quebec excluded itself) adds further protection to
Quebec in respect of language (sections 16-22) and
educational rights (section 23). The distinct society
clause seems to be nothing more than a recognition of an
established and historical fact. Quebec is indeed
different in respect to its laws, its language and its
culture.

There is the added fact that the Meech Lake
Accord in its other provisions confers on Quebec
additional rights beyond those granted to other provinces
-- for example in the matter of immigration and in
nominations to the Supreme Court (already dealt with in
preceding chapters of this analysis -- see chapters five
and six).

One wonders why there should be need for an additional statement of Quebec's distinctiveness, especially by use of such a term as "distinct society" which is vague and undefined. No one knows what those words really mean, or what additional powers will vest in Quebec beyond those already entrenched. The Accord gives to the government of Quebec and its legislature a role to "preserve and promote" the "distinct identity" of Quebec. No other province has been assigned a comparable role to promote its distinctiveness.

Prime Minister Mulroney has been quoted as saying that the distinct society clause does not mean much, that it is merely symbolic and is "nothing to worry about". If so, one wonders why it must be entrenched in the Constitution. Premier Bourassa of Quebec apparently views it differently, as having considerable significance for Quebecers. British Columbia's Premier Vander Zalm considers that all ten provinces and the two territories are "distinct" in their own particular way. He suggests that instead of a Quebec clause, we should have a "Canada Clause" proclaiming a "distinct national identity".

It would seem that Quebec's demand for recognition of its distinctiveness could have been met by a statement in the Preamble to the Accord, rather than by a substantive clause, designating Quebec as such. The effect would have been less threatening to minorities in Quebec, such as English-speaking citizens, natives and immigrants.

Without a clause in the Accord giving priority to the Canadian *Charter of Rights and Freedoms,* there is no assured protection of the rights granted in the *Charter* to all Canadians, wherever they live, in respect to language, education and multiculturalism (section 27). Some future Quebec government, in promoting its distinct identity could (for example) decide to eliminate

English schools, or restrict women's employment so as to preserve traditional French family life, or forbid the use of English in public institutions, government services or the media -- all in the cause of promoting Quebec's "distinct identity".

Another regrettable possibility would be that at some future time the government of Quebec might believe that to promote its distinct society or identity, it must become a separate state. The distinct identity clause could become the basis of renewed demands for independence.

Canadians are being told that denial to Quebec of its distinct society status would result in Quebec separating from Canada. Ironically however, that same clause, if carried to extreme, could produce the same result. For in promoting its distinct identity (which the Accord requires it to do), Quebec might interpret that as justifying a separate status, apart from Canada.

It is unfortunate for Quebec and for Canada that the distinct society clause has become the centre of so much controversy. Partly it is the result of the hastiness with which the Meech Lake Accord was negotiated, resulting in the use of a term which no one thought to define -- leading to differing interpretations and discord.

All this might have been avoided, or at least lessened, if the term "distinct society" had been placed in the Preamble to the Accord rather than in the text. There is reason to believe that this is what Quebec had in mind in the first place. However, once the distinct society status has become embodied in the text, Quebec is not likely to agree to its removal.

It is understandable that the objections now being voiced by some Canadians could be interpreted by Quebecers as a form of rejection, whereas in truth there is a genuine desire amongst Canadians to recognize

Quebec's distinctiveness. Our history, dating back to the Quebec Act of 1774, has shown a deference to Quebec's special needs. Perhaps this recognition can be achieved in ways less contentious than that attempted in the Meech Lake Accord.

In respect to language and culture we must not minimize the practical struggle which Quebec will always have with its 6-million population as it stands alone in a continent of 300 million where the main language is English. In that struggle which will be continuing into the future, Quebec stands in a stronger position within Canada, than outside Canada.

Maybe we have failed Quebec in the eyes of Quebecers, but it is hoped that they will join in the efforts which must be made now by all Canadians to ensure that Quebecers will see their future within the Canadian constitutional framework.

CHAPTER THIRTEEN

THE FRENCH/ENGLISH LANGUAGE PROVISION

WHAT THE ACCORD SAYS

In the same section as the distinct society clause, there is another clause -- section 2(1)(a) -- which recognizes "the existence of French-speaking Canadians centred in Quebec but also present elsewhere in Canada, and English-speaking Canadians concentrated outside Quebec but also present in Quebec".

There is nothing new in this -- simply a recognition of the French/English duality of our country -- except the statement that "the Constitution of Canada shall be interpreted in a manner consistent with the recognition" of this fact.

The section goes on to affirm [section 2(2)] that the role of both the Parliament of Canada and of the provincial legislatures is to "preserve" the English-speaking and French-speaking characteristic of Canada.

It will be noted that the word used here is "preserve" which means maintaining things as they are; there is no word "promote" (as with the distinct society clause). We can only assume then that French-speaking citizens residing outside Quebec, and English-speaking citizens residing inside Quebec (the minorities in each case) can expect nothing more than the status quo so far as their language rights are concerned. However, francophones in Quebec have the added benefit of the distinct society clause, in the promotion of which, the French language could be both "preserved and promoted".

Though some of these concerns may be resolved in the 1988 revisions to the *Official Languages Act,* francophones (in Alberta at least) say their position should be clarified not simply in an Act of Parliament, but in the constitution itself, which is the foundation of our law. They want to be assured of something more than just preserving the status quo, insofar as their francophone rights are concerned.

There is another feature about the Meech Lake provision on language. It speaks of "English-speaking" and "French-speaking" Canadians but nowhere does it mention Canadians who speak both English and French. The omission of any reference to bilingualism in the language provisions of the Meech Lake Accord could inhibit the continued development of bilingualism, which has been the official policy in Canada for over 25 years. It would seem that persons who master both languages will not fit exclusively into either category referred to in the Accord; or else they will fit into both.

QUEBEC'S LANGUAGE BILLS

Quebec's Bill 101, passed in 1978 (called "The Charter of the French Language") required all business signs throughout Quebec to be in the French language only (including posters, commercial signs and advertising). Two firms which used bilingual signs were charged with violations of this Act. They applied to the court for a declaration that they have the right to use the English language in their signs. The case eventually went to the Supreme Court of Canada -- reported in (1989) 36 Canadian Rights Reporter, pages 1, 64.

The Supreme Court on December 15, 1988 held that French-only signs are unconstitutional as infringing on the right to freedom of expression, which is contained in the Quebec "Charter of Rights and Freedoms" (section 3), and the "Canadian Charter of Rights and Freedoms" [section 2(b)]. The Court held that prohibition of other languages could not be justified as a means of promoting the French language. The Court held the attempted override law was defective in its wording.

Immediately following this, namely, on December 21, 1988, the government of Quebec circumvented the Supreme Court decision, and introduced Bill 178, the so-called "indoor-outdoor law", requiring French signs on the outside of business premises and limited English signs inside. To avoid this new law being challenged in court, as the earlier had been, Quebec made use of a revised provincial override law providing that Quebec statutes shall operate *notwithstanding* the fact that they may violate the Canadian *Charter of Rights*.

There was an immediate public reaction to what the Quebec government had done. It was seen as an affront to the Supreme Court of Canada. It was also seen as a suppression of the language rights of the English minority in Quebec. However, for whatever reason, Prime Minister Mulroney chose not to censure the Premier of Quebec. The immediate reaction of Manitoba Premier Gary Filmon was to officially repudiate the Meech Lake Accord, on which he had not, to that point, taken a definite stand.

THE NOTWITHSTANDING CLAUSE

Reference has been made to Quebec's use of its over-ride or "notwithstanding" clause in order to protect legislation from attack if it violates the *Charter of Rights*. The *Canadian Charter of Rights* contains a similar clause, and it has given rise to comment during the Meech Lake Debate. The clause in the *Charter* (section 33) allows legislatures or Parliament to declare that an Act shall operate "notwithstanding" the fact that it may violate rights protected by the *Charter*. It is well known that this clause was included in the *Charter* at the insistence of several provinces who made it their price for accepting the 1982 *Constitution Act*. During the debate over the Meech Lake Accord, Mr. Mulroney has been very critical of the "notwithstanding" clause, blaming the former Liberal government for its inclusion in the *Charter*. It is a matter of public record, however, that Mr. Mulroney (then in Opposition) supported the 1982 *Constitution Act* even though it contained the "notwithstanding" clause.

It is unfortunate to have such a clause in the *Charter,* but the Meech Lake Accord would have been an excellent opportunity to have it removed, when the premiers were in agreement on so many other issues. That was not done, and it will be very difficult to remove it in the future.

RECENT ATTACKS ON BILINGUALISM

Bilingualism has been Canada's official language policy since 1965. The intention of bilingualism was to give equal status to English and French, respecting language rights of English and French minorities, and encouraging each to learn the language of the other. While the policy has achieved some success, there have been a number of recent events which raise doubts about its continued efficacy. The following are some examples:

1. Several Ontario cities have declared themselves "English only", which means that services will be provided in the English language only. This was in reaction to Ontario Bill 8 *(French Language Services Act)* which would require provincial government services to be offered in both languages in designated areas where numbers warrant. Some persons regard this as a reaction to Quebec's sign law legislation.

2. The Supreme Court of Canada in April 1988 held that Saskatchewan provincial laws must be translated into French (based on an old territorial law). Alberta, to which this ruling would also apply, reacted by repealing the law, and enacting its own "Language Act" (July 6, 1988) which validated all previous Acts of the Alberta legislature, though not in French. Apparently the Alberta government was prepared to use the notwithstanding clause if the new Act was challenged (Jim Horsman, Inter-government Affairs Minister, speaking at the Men's Canadian Club in Edmonton, May 17, 1989).

3. The Northwest Territories Legislature in February 1990 expressed its objection to the *Official Languages Act* specifying English and French the sole languages for the Territories where only 5% of the population speak French. There are five native languages which, in the opinion of some legislators, deserve recognition.

Occurrences such as these have led many people to believe that bilingualism is not proving to be the unifying force it was intended to be, but instead has created an atmosphere of mistrust. Declaring "English-only cities" is hurtful to francophones, just as Quebec's Bill 178 barring English out-door signs is hurtful to anglophones. The Prime Minister has not chosen to speak out on any of these violations of minority-language protections.

What the Meech Lake Accord has done is replace bilingualism with the concept of "language duality" -- which could create two opposing enclaves, which may have difficulty in functioning harmoniously.

SUMMARY

The Meech Lake Accord preserves the French/English characteristic of Canada. It does not refer to bilingualism which has long been Canada's national policy. It seems to replace bilingualism by what might be termed "Language Duality". In other words, instead of a blending of languages, the effect of the Accord would be to treat the two languages as parallel.

It will be for Canadians to decide if this changed concept will be a unifying force, or if it will encourage linguistic conflict. Whatever the policy, political leadership is needed to ensure it is enforced.

CHAPTER FOURTEEN

CONCERNS OF WOMEN AND MINORITIES

These groups enjoy certain protections under the Canadian *Charter of Rights and Freedoms*. Concerns have been expressed, however, that the Meech Lake Accord contains no provision that the *Charter* takes precedence over the Accord. Without such a provision (clearly stated) there is no guarantee against these rights being over-ridden where a conflict arises between the *Charter* and the Accord.

For example, if the Quebec government, in promoting the "distinct identity" clause, found it necessary to encroach on the fundamental rights of certain Canadians, it is not clear how this could be prevented. Quebec could justify such action as part of its distinct society. There are a number of rights in the *Charter* that could be endangered in this way. The following are some examples:

(a) equality between males and females (section 28 of the *Charter*);

(b) equality before the law and equal protection and benefit of the law "without discrimination, and in particular, without discrimination based on race, national or ethnic origin, colour, religion, sex, age or mental or physical disability" (section 15);

(c) minority language educational rights (sections 23, 59) -- the right of certain children of French and

English background to receive education in their own language where numbers permit;

(d) mobility rights (section 6) -- the right to move to, reside in and gain employment in any province.

Unless the protections provided in the Canadian *Charter of Rights* have precedence over the Meech Lake Accord, then in the event of conflict between the two, some of these rights could be infringed. Many people view the omission of a general "priority" clause as a major flaw in the Meech Lake Accord.

This writer takes the position that section 2(4) of the Meech Lake Accord -- the non-derogation clause -- relates only to the powers and privileges of parliament and of the provincial legislatures under sections 91 and 92 of the *Constitution Act 1867* (and possibly section 93 relating to education).

A general clause at the end of the Meech Lake Accord (section 16) affords constitutional and *Charter* protection for specific groups and interests. Protected are: aboriginal and multicultural rights, Indians, and lands reserved for Indians. This means that these interests will be protected from the effects of section 2 of the Meech Lake Accord (the Distinct Society and language provisions).

The general rule for judicial interpretation is that where legislation contains specific exemptions, the latter represent the extent of exemptions. This would mean that other provisions of the Constitution and *Charter* are not exempt from the effects of section 2 of the Accord. The only way for other rights and freedoms to be protected (apart from those specifically mentioned in section 16) would be a clear general statement in the Accord giving precedence to the *Canadian Charter of Rights and Freedoms*. Without this, the rights listed above -- as (a), (b), (c), (d), -- will be in jeopardy.

The Meech Lake Accord

CHAPTER FIFTEEN

STATUS OF THE MEECH LAKE ACCORD
AS OF MARCH 1990

The Meech Lake Accord, which was signed by the Prime Minister and all ten provinces in June 1987, had to be ratified by Parliament and by all the provincial legislatures in order to become law.

The necessary resolution was passed without difficulty by Parliament, and by eight of the ten provincial legislatures. However, New Brunswick and Manitoba have refused to ratify the Accord.

More recently, Premier Clyde Wells of Newfoundland (himself an able constitutional lawyer) has threatened to withdraw the ratification given by the former Conservative government of Brian Peckford. For a time, in January 1990, B.C. Premier Vander Zalm threatened to do the same, saying the Accord was unacceptable to the people of his province. However, he has since indicated that he will not withdraw his province's ratification, despite what he describes as his "reticence" about it.

The status of the Meech Lake Accord as of March 1990 is this: the premiers of Manitoba and New Brunswick are maintaining their positions that they will not ratify the Accord without major amendments. The premier of Newfoundland is taking the same position, and may even revoke his province's earlier ratification.

The final date for ratification by all provinces has been set at June 23, 1990 (being three years following ratification by the Province of Quebec). Failing approval by that time, the Accord will die.

CHAPTER SIXTEEN

GROUPS SUPPORTING THE MEECH LAKE ACCORD

Over the next few months, Canadians will likely be besieged with a barrage of propaganda from the federal government, academics and influential business leaders urging support for the Meech Lake Accord. These groups are similar in their categories to those which supported the Free Trade Agreement. Because of abundant financial resources, they are able to exert considerable influence. One such group calls itself "Friends of Meech Lake".

CHAPTER SEVENTEEN

THE FEDERAL GOVERNMENT POSITION

Even though there was no public consultation on the Meech Lake Accord before it was signed, the federal government has maintained its position from the beginning that the Accord will not be changed in any aspect. Yet the Canadian public had no part in its formulation.

Despite growing opposition, both Mr. Mulroney and Premier Bourassa have flatly rejected any amendments, while threatening dire consequences if the Accord fails. They appear to have adopted an "all-or-nothing" attitude. As recently as February 3, 1990, Mr. Mulroney, speaking in Montreal, in a vibrant plea for the Accord, called it "a statement of love of Canada". In response, New Brunswick Premier Frank McKenna, who was in attendance, said that while the stakes are high, "Canada's future will be even more shaky if the Accord is adopted *without* change".

CHAPTER EIGHTEEN

ALTERNATIVES TO THE MEECH LAKE ACCORD

No viable alternatives have proven acceptable for breaking the impasse over the Meech Lake Accord.

Proposals have come forward from two premiers, both of whom signed the Accord. In January 1990, Premier Vander Zalm of British Columbia, proposed that the Accord be implemented in two stages: first, those parts satisfying the present amending formula could be proclaimed by the deadline date of June 23, 1990; second, other parts of the Accord which require unanimous consent could be delayed, with a time limit set for further negotiations. Neither the Prime Minister nor his colleague, Senator Lowell Murray (Minister for Federal-Provincial Relations) showed much interest in this proposal. One of Premier Vander Zalm's suggestions was that all ten provinces and the two Territories be declared distinct societies.

On February 5, 1990, Ontario Premier David Peterson, speaking in Quebec City alluded to his own proposal which would ratify the Accord, and then proceed to further negotiations. With the Meech Lake Accord in place, however, the unanimity rule on further changes would apply.

Another suggestion which has been made is for a so-called "Parallel Accord", first proposed by New Brunswick Premier McKenna, but no group has developed or formalized the concept. Whatever its merits, the Prime Minister and Quebec Premier Bourassa have made it clear that the Meech Lake Accord must first be passed in its present form. Once that were done, any major changes would require unanimous consent. There is little hope that all provinces would agree on controversial issues which they could not resolve before. The euphoria of June 1987 when all premiers so readily achieved unanimity was a short-lived miracle.

A Parallel Accord could not hope to address the deficiencies in the Meech Lake Accord without re-writing it: such concerns, for example, as those affecting minorities, aboriginals, women, new provinces and the veto. These items are all too important to be relegated to a secondary or "parallel accord", and would only add to the confusion.

Still another suggestion is to let the Meech Lake Accord die, and immediately begin new constitutional talks. After all, this was the fate of the Victoria Constitutional Charter of 1971 which was passed, then renounced by Quebec, leading to another decade of negotiations before the new Constitution was approved in 1982 (though once again not ratified by Quebec).

Changes in a nation's constitution are of necessity slow. The attempt at Meech Lake to accelerate the process in secret without public participation was bound to produce the situation that now confronts Canadians.

CHAPTER NINETEEN

CONSEQUENCES OF REJECTING THE ACCORD

It is unfortunate that the federal government (and some media) have promoted the idea that rejection of the Meech Lake Accord is a rejection of Quebec.

Canadians are being told by political leaders that if the Accord is not ratified, Quebec will separate from Canada. However, the same result could occur even if the Accord were ratified. Some future Quebec government might take the position that the promotion of Quebec's "distinct identity" necessitates separation. So, whether the Accord is accepted or rejected, the result could be the same in the end. Rejecting the Accord, or accepting it with its distinct society clause, could eventually produce the same unfortunate result. It is the Accord itself that has produced this dilemma.

Canadians outside Quebec do not want to say "No" to Quebec, yet political leaders portray acceptance or rejection in that light. The distinct status of Quebec is only one of several features about the Accord that are controversial.

Quebec enjoys many advantages by being part of Canada -- much more than if it were to drift under American domination. If it became a separate country, it would require its own defence forces (army, navy and air-force), its own currency, banking system and financial structure, postal system, social services, international treaties and foreign embassies -- which would be very costly for a sovereign state with only six million people.

It is reasonable to expect that most Quebecers will choose not to take the separation route, and that a constitutional arrangement can be reached which will take into account the interest of all Canadians, inside and outside Quebec.

Canadians should not allow themselves to be intimidated by warnings, threats, and ultimatums, but instead we should direct attention to the question: What will the Meech Lake Accord mean for Canada?

CHAPTER TWENTY

SUMMARY AND CONCLUSIONS

The weakness of the Meech Lake Accord lies not only in what it has done, but in how it has done it.

SUMMARY

The process

The process from the start has been undemocratic. It began with eleven men meeting in secret to radically change the Canadian constitution, but with no mandate from the public to do so. Nor was there any information made available in advance as to what was being discussed. When Canadians were presented with the final document -- the Meech Lake Accord -- they were told it cannot be altered: no changes are possible; it must be accepted as it is. Despite nearly three years of discussion and debate, the federal government continues to hold to that position.

The content

As to the content of the Accord, it represents a radical shift of power from the federal government to the provincial governments. The original purpose of the Accord was to satisfy the demands which Quebec made as its condition for agreeing to sign the 1982 *Constitution* (from which it had earlier exempted itself).

To gain agreement from the other nine premiers to concessions being granted to Quebec, the federal government gave similar powers to all the provinces. Because these are powers which properly belong at the federal level of government, the result will be weakening of the national fabric.

The issues

The powers which would pass to the Provinces under the Meech Lake Accord include:

1. greater provincial control over immigration;

2. provincial government nominations to the Senate;

3. provincial government nominations for Judges of the Supreme Court of Canada;

4. greater provincial control over federal spending on shared-cost programs, including the right of provinces to opt out and receive compensation.

5. a veto to all provinces on major constitutional amendments in future.

If the Accord is ratified, the chances of achieving Senate reform are almost nonexistent. On such a contentious issue, uniformity among the provinces would be almost impossible to achieve, since the veto of just one province could defeat any proposal.

A serious defect in the Meech Lake Accord is its failure to give precedence to the Canadian *Charter of Rights and Freedoms*. Without such a provision, clearly stated, the rights of women, minorities, natives and northern Canadians could be at risk in future.

While much publicity has centred on the special status granted to Quebec as a "distinct society", this is only one of several issues that are controversial about the Meech Lake Accord. That subject, and all the topics mentioned above, are discussed at length in earlier Chapters of this analysis.

The impasse

There seems to be no option out of the impasse that has been created. It is the Accord itself that has produced the impasse -- both by the process that created it, and the intractable position maintained by the federal government since.

One suggestion has been for a Parallel Accord. However, both the federal and Quebec governments have made it clear that no such proposal could be considered until after the Meech Lake Accord is ratified. This means that the unanimity rule would then be in effect, and a single veto could defeat any proposal.

A Parallel Accord could not address the deficiencies in the Meech Lake Accord without actually re-writing it. Concerns of minorities, aboriginals, women and the northern territories are too important to be relegated to a secondary or "parallel" accord.

The choices

If the Meech Lake Accord is ratified, it would mean that instead of a united Canada, we would have a fragmented country, each province being semi-autonomous, and each premier with enhanced powers. Yet these are times when Canada needs a strong central government to maintain a sense of national purpose, to alleviate economic disparities and to arbitrate regional differences. Never before has Canada been more in need of a united system of government with power to cope with the serious economic, social and environmental concerns facing us as a nation.

If the Meech Lake Accord is rejected, we will begin again -- however long it may take -- to achieve a better Accord which will address Quebec's special needs, and at the same time assure for all Canadians a strong unified country.

CONCLUSION

We are unhappily confronted with a difficult choice. Above all else, we must not allow our country to be tied into a system which cannot readily be changed and which could remain with us for years to come -- even forever.

This analysis has endeavoured to present the facts so that Canadians everywhere can participate in the final resolution of this dilemma. The question for all to ponder is this: What are the long-term implications of the Meech Lake Accord? If it threatens our solidarity as a nation, we must demand something better for ourselves and for future generations of Canadians.

ADDENDUM
WHAT WE AS CANADIANS CAN DO

1. Become informed. Express opinions to politicians and others. Let it be known how much is involved in the Meech Lake Accord, and how serious are the consequences.

2. Insist that the debate extend beyond Quebec's demands to the concerns of Canadians everywhere. Assure proper attention is given to the views of other provinces and of the Territories as to the effect of the Accord on them.

3. Discourage attempts by the federal government to force compliance from the governments of Manitoba, New Brunswick and Newfoundland. Allow these provinces freedom of choice.

4. Without some clear indication of consensus being reached, require that the impasse over the Accord be acknowledged now, to end the acrimony, rather than waiting for the June 23 deadline.

5. Using the Meech Lake Accord as a draft, insist that discussions begin immediateley between the federal and provincial governments, along the following lines:

   (a). Acknowledge Quebec's legitimate demands, but make the promotion of its "distinct identity" subject to the Canadian *Charter of Rights and Freedoms.*

   (b). have the veto power limited to Quebec alone, and to be applied only where its interests are directly affected.

   (c). immediately address the concerns of the Northwest Territories and the Yukon (explained in Chapter 9).

(d). require the 9 premiers, outside Quebec, to give up some of the powers granted to them under the Meech Lake Accord. Unless this is done, Canada could disintegrate into 10 semi-autonomous principalities, with a national government unable to fulfill its unifying role for all Canadians.

CONCLUDING COMMENT

In the long run, the weakness of the Meech Lake Accord may lie less in what has been granted to Quebec than in the unwise extension of powers to the other nine provinces.

Most of the added powers given to the nine premiers, outside Quebec, properly belong to a national government. Transfer of these powers was partly aimed at procuring consent of those premiers to the arrangement with Quebec. All of the nine premiers at the time accepted these new powers. However, the three provinces (New Brunswick, Manitoba and Newfoundland) which have elected new governments since the 1987 Meech Lake Accord have expressed strong objections to it. Their suggestions for amendment, however have been rejected.

The federal government has taken the position that any form of "Parallel Accord" will not be considered until *after* the Meech Lake Accord is ratified. The new amending rule of unanimity will then apply, with little probability of agreement on unresolved issues.

In the light of this, it would be appropriate in the interest of a united Canada if the other six provinces (British Columbia, Alberta, Saskatchewan, Ontario, Nova Scotia, Prince Edward Island) to reconsider their position and relinquish some of the powers which were unwisely given to them under the Meech Lake Accord. Far worse than two Canadas would be ten.

- The Author March 25, 1990

ABOUT THE AUTHOR

Biographical Sketch of

MARJORIE MONTGOMERY BOWKER

Graduated in Law from the University of Alberta. Admitted to the Alberta Bar. Practised with the Edmonton law firm of Milner Steer.

1966 - Appointed Judge of the Provincial Court of Alberta, Family and Juvenile Divisions. Served in that capacity for 17 years, retiring in 1983.

RECENT PUBLISHED WRITINGS

1986 - "Juvenile Court in Retrospect: Seven Decades of History in Alberta (1913 - 1984)" (*Alberta Law Review*, 1986, Volume 24).

1987 - "Waiver of Juveniles to Adult court under the Juveniles Delinquents Act: Applicability of Principles to the Young Offenders Act" (*Criminal Law Quarterly*, 1987, Volume 29) (Note: This article was cited with approval in both the majority and dissenting judgments in a case before the Supreme Court of Canada, September 1989).

1988 - *On Guard for Thee* -an independent review of the Free Trade Agreement (published by

Voyageur Publishing, Hull, Quebec) - a national best seller.

1989- Editor, *Fifty Years of Legal Writings of W.F. Bowker (1938 - 1988)* - published by University of Alberta Press.

HONOURS AND AWARDS

1968 - Honourary Degree, Doctor of Laws, Ewha Women's University, Seoul, Korea.

1978 - Queen Elizabeth Silver Jubilee Medal.

1981 - Alberta Achievement Award.

1983 - Award of Merit, American Association of Family Conciliation courts.

1989 - Woman of the Year Award, Business and Professional Women's Club of Edmonton.
- YWCA Tribute to Women Award.
- Distinguished Canadian Award - Council of Canadians, presented in Ottawa, October 1989.

Marjorie Bowker is the wife of Wilbur F. Bowker, now retired, who was for 20 years Dean of Law at the University of Alberta. The Bowkers will be celebrating their 50th wedding anniversary this year. They have three adult children, one in Alberta and two in Ontario - all in the health-care field. There are 7 grandchildren.

TEXT OF THE MEECH LAKE ACCORD:

1987 CONSTITUTIONAL ACCORD
(COMPLETE TEXT)

JUNE 3, 1987

WHEREAS first ministers, assembled in Ottawa, have arrived at a unanimous accord on constitutional amendments that would bring about the full and active participation of Quebec in Canada's constitutional evolution, would recognize the principle of equality of all provinces, would provide new arrangements to foster greater harmony and cooperation between the Government of Canada and the governments of the provinces and would require that annual constitutional conferences composed of first ministers be convened not later than December 31, 1988;

AND WHEREAS first ministers have also reached unanimous agreement on certain additional commitments in relation to some of those amendments;

NOW THEREFORE the Prime Minister of Canada and the first ministers of the provinces commit themselves and the governments they represent to the following:

1. The Prime Minister of Canada will lay or cause to be laid before the Senate and House of Commons, and the first ministers of the provinces will lay or cause to be laid before their legislative assemblies, as soon as possible, a resolution, in the form appended hereto, to authorize a proclamation to be issued by the Governor General under the Great Seal of Canada to amend the Constitution of Canada.

2. The Government of Canada will, as soon as possible, conclude an agreement with the Government of Quebec that would

(a) incorporate the principles of the Cullen-Couture agreement on the selection abroad and in Canada of independent immigrants, visitors for medical treatment, students and temporary workers, and on the selection of refugees abroad and economic criteria for family reunification and assisted relatives,

(b) guarantee that Quebec will receive a number of immigrants, including refugees, within the annual total established by the federal government for all of Canada proportionate to its share of the population of Canada, with the right to exceed that figure by five per cent for demographic reasons, and

(c) provide an undertaking by Canada to withdraw services (except citizenship services) for the reception and integration (including linguistic and cultural) of all foreign nationals wishing to settle in Quebec where services are to be provided by Quebec, with such withdrawal to be accompanied by reasonable compensation,

and the Government of Canada and the Government of Quebec will take the necessary steps to give the agreement the force of law under the proposed amendment relating to such agreements.

3. Nothing in this Accord should be construed as preventing the negotiation of similar agreements with other provinces relating to immigration and the temporary admission of aliens.

4. Until the proposed amendment relating to appointments to the Senate comes into force, any person summoned to fill a vacancy in the Senate shall be chosen from among persons whose names have been submitted by the government of the province to which the vacancy relates and must be acceptable to the Queen's Privy Council for Canada.

Motion for a Resolution to authorize
an amendment to the Constitution of Canada

WHEREAS the Constitution Act, 1982 came into force on April 17, 1982, following an agreement between Canada and all the provinces except Quebec;

AND WHEREAS the Government of Quebec has established a set of five proposals for constitutional change and has stated that amendments to give effect to those proposals would enable Quebec to resume a full role in the constitutional councils of Canada;

AND WHEREAS the amendment proposed in the schedule hereto sets out the basis on which Quebec's five constitutional proposals may be met;

AND WHEREAS the amendment proposed in the schedule hereto also recognizes the principle of the equality of all the provinces, provides new arrangements to foster greater harmony and cooperation between the Government of Canada and the governments of the provinces and requires that conferences be convened to consider important constitutional, economic and other issues;

AND WHEREAS certain portions of the amendment proposed in the schedule hereto relate to matters referred to in section 41 of the Constitution Act, 1982;

AND WHEREAS section 41 of the Constitution Act, 1982 provides that an amendment to the Constitution of Canada may be made by proclamation issued by the Governor General under the Great Seal of Canada where so authorized by resolutions of the Senate and the House of Commons and of the legislative assembly of each province;

NOW THEREFORE the (Senate) (House of Commons) (legislative assembly) resolves that an amendment to the Constitution of Canada be authorized to be made by proclamation issued by Her Excellency the Governor General under the Great Seal of Canada in accordance with the schedule hereto.

SCHEDULE

CONSTITUTION AMENDMENT, 1987

Constitution Act, 1867

1. The *Constitution Act, 1867* is amended by adding thereto, immediately after section 1 thereof, the following section:

Interpretation

2. (1) The Constitution of Canada shall be interpreted in a manner consistent with

(*a*) the recognition that the existence of French-speaking Canadians, centered in Quebec but also present elsewhere in Canada, and English-speaking Canadians, concentrated outside Quebec but also present in Quebec, constitutes a fundamental characteristic of Canada; and

(*b*) the recognition that Quebec constitutes within Canada a distinct society.

Role of Parliament and legislatures

(2) The role of the Parliament of Canada and the provincial legislatures to preserve the fundamental characteristic of Canada referred to in paragraph (1) (*a*) is affirmed.

Role of legislature and Government of Quebec

(3) The role of the legislature and Government of Quebec to preserve and promote the distinct identity of Quebec referred to in paragraph (1) (*b*) is affirmed.

Rights of leg-

(4) Nothing in this section derogates from the

The Meech Lake Accord   8 3

islatures and governments preserved

powers, rights or privileges of Parliament or the Government of Canada, or of the legislatures or governments of the provinces, including any powers, rights or privileges relating to language.

2. The said Act is further amended by adding thereto, immediately after section 24 thereof, the following section:

Names to be submitted

25. (1) Where a vacancy occurs in the Senate, the government of the province to which the vacancy relates may, in relation to that vacancy, submit to the Queen's Privy Council for Canada the names of persons who may be summoned to the Senate.

Choice of Senators from names submitted

(2) Until an amendment to the Constitution of Canada is made in relation to the Senate pursuant to section 41 of the *Constitution Act, 1982*, the person summoned to fill a vacancy in the Senate shall be chosen from among persons whose names have been submitted under subsection (1) by the government of the province to which the vacancy relates and must be acceptable to the Queen's Privy Council for Canada.

3. The said Act is further amended by adding thereto, immediately after section 95 thereof, the following heading and sections:

Agreements on Immigration and Aliens

Commitment to negotiate

95A. The Government of Canada shall, at the request of the government of any province, negotiate with the government of that province for the purpose of concluding an agreement relating to immigration or the temporary admission of aliens into that province that is appropriate to the needs and circumstances of that province.

Agreements

95B. (1) Any agreement concluded between Canada and a province in relation to immigration or the temporary admission of aliens into that province has the force of law from the time it is declared to do so in accordance with subsection 95C (1) and shall from that time have effect notwithstanding class 25 of section 91 or section 95.

Limitation

(2) An agreement that has the force of law under

The Meech Lake Accord

subsection (1) shall have effect only so long and so far as it is not repugnant to any provision of an Act of the Parliament of Canada that sets national standards and objectives relating to immigration or aliens, including any provision that establishes general classes of immigrants or relates to levels of immigration for Canada or that prescribes classes of individuals who are inadmissible into Canada.

Application of Charter

(3) The *Canadian Charter of Rights and Freedoms* applies in respect of any agreement that has the force of law under subsection (1) and in respect of anything done by the Parliament or Government of Canada, or the legislature or government of a province, pursuant to any such agreement.

Proclamation relating to agreements

95C. (1) A declaration that an agreement referred to in subsection 95S(1) has the force of law may be made by proclamation issued by the Governor General under the Great Seal of Canada only where so authorized by resolutions of the Senate and House of Commons and of the legislative assembly of the province that is a party to the agreement.

Amendment of agreements

(2)An amendment to an agreement referred to in subsection 95B(1) may be made by proclamation issued by the Governor General under the Great Seal of Canada only where so authorized

(a) by resolutions of the Senate and House of Commons and of the legislative assembly of the province that is a party to the agreement; or

(b) in such other manner as is set out in the agreement.

Application of sections 46 to 48 of *Constitution Act, 1982*

95D. Sections 46 to 48 of the *Constitution Act, 1982* apply, with such modifications as the circumstances require, in respect of any declaration made pursuant to subsection 95C(1), any amendment to an agreement made pursuant to subsection 95C(2) or any amendment made pursuant to section 95E.

Amendments to Sections

95E. An amendment to sections 95A to 95D of this section may be made in accordance with the

95A to 95D or this section	procedure set out in subsection 38(1) of the *Constitution Act, 1982*, but only if the amendment is authorized by resolutions of the legislative assemblies of all the provinces that are, at the time of the amendment, parties to an agreement that has the force of law under subsection 95B(1).

4. The said Act is further amended by adding thereto, immediately preceding section 96 thereof, the following heading:

General

5. The said Act is further amended by adding thereto, immediately preceding section 101 thereof, the following heading:

Courts Established by the Parliament of Canada

6. The said Act is further amended by adding thereto, immediately after section 10 1 thereof, the following heading and sections:

Supreme Court of Canada

Supreme Court continued	**101A.** (1) The court existing under the name of the Supreme Court of Canada is hereby continued as the general court of appeal for Canada, and as an additional court for the better administration of the laws of Canada, and shall continue to be a superior court of record.
Constitution of Court	(2) The Supreme Court of Canada shall consist of a chief justice to be called the Chief Justice of Canada and eight other judges, who shall be appointed by the Governor General in Council by letters patent under the Great Seal.
Who may be appointed been judges	**101B.** (1) Any person may be appointed a judge of the Supreme Court of Canada who after having admitted to the bar of any province or territory, has, for a total of at least ten years, been a judge of any courts in Canada or a member of the bar of any province or territory.
Three judges from Quebec	(2) At least three judges of the Supreme Court of Canada shall be appointed from among

The Meech Lake Accord

persons who, after having been admitted to the bar of Quebec, have, for a total of at least ten years, been judges of any court of Quebec or of any court established by the Parliament of Canada, or members of the bar of Quebec.

Names may be submitted

1O1C. (1) Where a vacancy occurs in the Supreme Court of Canada, the government of each province may, in relation to that vacancy, submit to the Minister of Justice of Canada the names of any of the persons who have been admitted to the bar of that province and are qualified under section 1O1B for appointment to that Court.

Appointment from names submitted

(2) Where an appointment is made to the Supreme Court of Canada, the Governor General in Council shall, except where the Chief Justice is appointed from among members of the Court, appoint a person whose name has been submitted under subsection (1) and who is acceptable to the Queen's Privy Council for Canada.

Appointment from Quebec

(3)Where an appointment is made in accordance with subsection (2) of any of the three judges necessary to meet the requirement set out in subsection 1O1B(2), the Governor General in Council shall appoint a person whose name has been submitted by the Government of Quebec.

Appointment from other provinces

(4)Where an appointment is made in accordance with subsection (2) otherwise than as required under subsection (3), the Governor General in Council shall appoint a person whose name has been submitted by the government of a province other than Quebec.

Tenure, salaries, etc. of judges

101D. Sections 99 and 100 apply in respect of judges of the Supreme Court of Canada.

Relationship to section 101

1O1E. (1) Sections 101A to 1O1D shall not be construed as abrogating or derogating from the powers of the parliament of Canada to make laws under section 101 except to the extent that such laws are inconsistent with those sections.

References to the Supreme

(2) For greater certainty, section 101A shall not be construed as abrogating or derogating

Court of Canada | from the powers of the Parliament of Canada to make laws relating to the reference of questions of law or fact, or any other matters, to the Supreme Court of Canada.

7. The said Act is further amended by adding thereto, immediately after section 106 thereof, the following section:

Shared-cost program | **106A** (1) The Government of Canada shall provide reasonable compensation to the government of a province that chooses not to participate in a national shared cost program that is established by the Government of Canada after the coming into force of this section in an area of exclusive provincial jurisdiction, if the province carries on a program or initiative that is compatible with the national objectives.

Legislative power not extended | (2) Nothing in this section extends the legislative powers of the Parliament of Canada or of the legislatures of the provinces.

8. The said Act is further amended by adding thereto the following heading and sections:

XII -CONFERENCES ON THE ECONOMY AND OTHER MATTERS

Conferences on the economy and other matters | **148.** A conference composed of the Prime Minister of Canada and the first ministers of the provinces shall be convened by the Prime Minister of Canada at least once each year to discuss the state of the Canadian economy and such other matters as may be appropriate.

XIII -REFERENCES

Reference includes amendments | **149.** A reference to this Act shall be deemed to include a reference to any amendments thereto.

Constitution Act, 1982

9. Sections 40 to 42 of the *Constitution Act, 1982* are repealed and the following substituted therefor:

Compensation | **40.** Where an amendment is made under subsection

38(1) that transfers legislative powers from provincial legislatures to Parliament, Canada shall provide reasonable compensation to any province to which the amendment does not apply.

Amendment by unanimous consent

41. An amendment to the Constitution of Canada in relation to the following matters may be made by proclamation issued by the Governor General under the Great Seal of Canada only where authorized by resolutions of the Senate and House of Commons and of the legislative assembly of each province:

(a) the office of the Queen, the Governor General and the Lieutenant Governor of a province;

(b) the powers of the Senate and the method of selecting Senators;

(c) the number of members by which a province is entitled to be represented in the Senate and the residence qualifications of Senators;

(d) the right of a province to a number of members in the House of Commons not less than the number of Senators by which the province was entitled to be represented on *April 17, 1982*;

(e) the principle of proportionate representation of the provinces in the House of Commons prescribed by the Constitution of Canada;

(f) subject to section 43, the use of the English or the French language;

(g) the Supreme Court of Canada;

(h) the extension of existing provinces into the territories;

(i) notwithstanding any other law or practice, the establishment of new provinces; and

(j) an amendment to this Part.

10. Section 44 of the said Act is repealed and the following substituted therefor:

Amendments
by Parliament

44. Subject to section 4 1, Parliament may exclusively make laws amending the Constitution of Canada in relation to the executive government of Canada or the Senate and House of Commons.

11. Subsection 46(1) of the said Act is repealed and the following substituted there for:

Initiation of
amendment
procedures

46.(1) The procedures for amendment under sections 38, 41, and 43 may be initiated either by the Senate or the House of Commons or by the legislative assembly of a province.

12. Subsection 47(1) of the said Act is repealed and the following substituted there for:

Amendments
without
Senate
resolution

47.(1) An amendment to the Constitution of Canada made by proclamation under section 38, 41 or 43 may be made without a resolution of the Senate authorizing the issue of the proclamation if, within one hundred and eighty days after the adoption by the House of Commons of a resolution authorizing its issue, the Senate has not adopted such a resolution and if, at any time after the expiration of that period, the House of Commons again adopts the resolution.

13. Part VI of the said Act is repealed and the following substituted therefor:

PART VI

CONSTITUTIONAL CONFERENCES

Constitutional
conference

50. (1) A constitutional conference composed of the Prime Minister of Canada and the first ministers of the provinces shall be convened by the Prime Minister of Canada at least once each year, commencing in 1988.

Agenda

(2) The conferences convened under subsection (1) shall have included on their agenda the following matters:

(a) Senate reform, including the role and functions of the Senate, its powers, the method of selecting Senators and representation in the Senate;

(b) roles and responsibilities in relation to fisheries; and

(c) such other matters as are agreed upon.

14. Subsection 52(2) of the said Act is amended by striking out the word "and" at the end of paragraph (b) thereof, by adding the word "and" at the end of paragraph (c) thereof and by adding thereto the following paragraph:

(d) any other amendment to the Constitution of Canada.

15. Section 61 of the said Act is repealed and the following substituted there for:

References

61. A reference to the *Constitution Act 1982*, or a reference to the *Constitution Acts 1867 to 1982*, shall be deemed to include a reference to any amendments thereto.

General

Multi-cultural heritage and aboriginal peoples

16. Nothing in Section 2 of the Constitution Act, 1867 affects section 25 or 27 of the Canadian Charter of Rights and Freedoms, section 35 of the Constitution Act, 1982 or class 24 of section 91 of the Constitution Act 1867.

CITATION

Citation

17. This amendment may be cited as the *Constitution Amendment, 1987.*

THE POLITICAL ACCORD

MEECH LAKE COMMUNIQUE

(COMPLETE TEXT)

OF APRIL 30, 1987

At their meeting today at Meech Lake, the Prime Minister and the ten Premiers agreed to ask officials to transform into a constitutional text the agreement in principle found in the attached document.

First Ministers also agreed to hold a constitutional conference within weeks to approve a formal text intended to allow Quebec to resume its place as a full participant in Canada's constitutional development.

QUEBEC'S DISTINCT SOCIETY

(1)   The Constitution of Canada shall be interpreted in a manner consistent with
   a)   the recognition that the existence of French-speaking Canada, centered in but not limited to Quebec, and English-speaking Canada, concentrated outside Quebec but also present in Quebec, constitutes a fundamental characteristic of Canada; and
   b)   the recognition that Quebec constitutes within Canada a distinct society.

(2)   Parliament and the provincial legislatures, in the exercise of their respective powers, are committed to preserving the fundamental characteristic of Canada referred to in paragraph (1)(a).

(3)   The role of the legislature and Government of Quebec to preserve and promote the distinct identity of Quebec referred to in paragraph (1)(b) is affirmed.

IMMIGRATION

- Provide under the Constitution that the Government of Canada shall negotiate an immigration agreement appropriate to the needs and circumstances of a province that so requests and that, once concluded, the agreement may by entrenched at the request of the province;

- Such agreements must recognize the federal government's power to set national standards and objectives relating to immigration, such as the ability to determine general categories of immigrants, to establish overall levels of immigration and prescribe categories of inadmissible persons;

- under the foregoing provisions, conclude in the first instance an agreement with Quebec that would:

* incorporate the principles of the Cullen-Couture agreement on the selection abroad and in Canada of independent immigrants, visitors for medical treatment, students and temporary workers, and on the selection of refugees abroad and economic criteria for family reunification and assist relatives.

* guarantee that Quebec will receive a number of immigrants, including refugees, within the annual total established by the federal government for all of Canada proportionate to its share of the population of Canada, with the right to exceed that figure by 5% for demographic reasons; and

* provide an undertaking by Canada to withdraw services (except citizenship services) for the reception and integration (including linguistic and cultural) of all foreign nationals wishing to settle in Quebec where services are to be provided by Quebec, with such withdrawal to be accompanied by reasonable compensation;

- nothing in the foregoing should be construed as preventing the negotiation of similar agreements with other provinces.

SUPREME COURT OF CANADA

- Entrench the Supreme Court and the requirement that at least three of the nine justices appointed be from the civil bar;

- provide that, where there is a vacancy on the supreme Court, the federal government shall appoint a person from a list of candidates proposed by the provinces and who is acceptable to the federal government.

SPENDING POWER

- Stipulate that Canada must provide reasonable compensation to any province that does not participate in a future national shared-cost program in an area of exclusive provincial jurisdiction if that province undertakes its own initiative on programs compatible with national objectives.

AMENDING FORMULA

- Maintain the current general amending formula set out in section 38, which requires the consent of Parliament and at least two-thirds of the provinces representing at least fifty percent of the population;

- guarantee reasonable compensation in all cases where a province opts out of an amendment transferring provincial jurisdiction to parliament;

- because opting out of constitutional amendments to matters set out in section 42 of the *Constitution Act, 1982* is not possible, require the consent of Parliament and all the provinces for such amendments.

SECOND ROUND

- Require that a First Ministers' Conference on the Constitution be held not less than once per year and that the first be held within twelve months of proclamation of this amendment but not later than the end of 1988;

- entrench in the Constitution the following items on the agenda:
  1) Senate reform including
     -the functions and role of the Senate;
     -the powers of the Senate;
     -the method of selection of Senators;
     -the distribution of Senate seats;
  2) fisheries roles and responsibilities; and
  3) other agreed upon matters;

- entrench in the Constitution the annual First Ministers' Conference on the Economy now held under the terms of the February 1985 Memorandum of the Agreement;

- until constitutional amendments regarding the Senate are accomplished the federal government shall appoint persons from lists of candidates provided by provinces where vacancies occur and who are acceptable to the federal government.

Other Books on National Issues
by Voyageur Publishing
Available Now

On Guard For Thee, Marjorie Bowker

An independent review of the Free Trade Agreement by the same author as this book. A National Best-Seller in Paperback.

Suggested Retail $4.95

Meech Lake Reconsidered, Edited by Lorne Ingle QC

A Collection of articles on the Meech Lake Accord by:
The Hon. Allan Blakeney (Former Premier of Saskatchewan 1971-1982), The Hon. Eugene Forsey (Research Director CCL & CLC 1940-70, Senator 1970-79), Prof. Howard McConnell (College of Law, University of Saskatchewan), The Hon. Tony Penikett (Yukon Government Leader), Prof. Andrew J. Petter (Faculty of Law University of Victoria), Prof. Donald J. Purich (Director, Native Law Centre University of Saskatchewan), Dr. Bryan Schwartz (University of Manitoba), Dean John D. Whyte (Faculty of Law Queen's University).
Includes the complete text of The Meech Lake Accord 1987, The Political Accord 1987, The *Constitution Act 1982*, The *Charter of Rights and Freedoms*, The *Constitution Act 1867* (The BNA Act).

Suggested Retail $5.95

Retreat From Governance, Prof. H.T. Wilson

A York University Professor, Wilson traces the retreat from traditional patterns and obligations of governance by the Canadian federal government over the past decade. This process has accelerated massively since the election of Brian Mulroney in 1984. The major effect of this retreat is the displacement of complementary Canadian institutions by miniature-replica American ones. Wilson illustrates his thesis with the following examples:
> the Free Trade Agreement;
> privatization of public enterprises;
> withdrawal or curtailment of public services and benefits;
> the attack on the universality principle;
> misinformation about the public debt;
> patriation and entrenchment (1982);
> the Meech Lake Accord;
> Senate reform;
> the office of Prime Minister; and
> reform of the House of Commons.

Wilson argues that Canadian autonomy is at stake in this wholesale abandonment of Canadian institutions and practises.

Suggested Retail $9.95

Coming Soon From
Voyageur Publishing
More Important Books on National Issues

Not A Sentimental Journey (2nd Edition), Jo Davis

The author charges that the latest VIA cuts are a part of a long-term strategy that is nothing more than a conspiracy designed to destroy passenger rail in Canada. She documents cases of incompetence and damage by design on the part of our decision makers and how years of neglect on the part of the federal government have taken their toll on passenger rail. This book puts to rest the myths that Canadians don't want trains and that passenger rail is out-dated and not practical in the 1990's. The author proves that Canadians do want the trains, do use the trains, and are mad that they are being stolen from them. This book is in an accessible format that includes reprinted articles and political cartoons interlaced by the author's commentary. Of particular interest is her argument that this decision flies in the face of environmental responsibility. The author claims that the only difference between Communist propaganda and our own is that they don't believe theirs anymore.

---

39 Days In Hell, Paul Vidosa, ex-RCMP Agent.

This is the true story of a Canadian agent who was convicted to serving five years in a Colombian jail without trial while working undercover for the RCMP. For 39 days, he remained captive where he was beaten and tortured. On January 9, 1981 the Medellin Drug Cartel, the subject of his investigations, paid the $75,000 U.S. demanded by his captors. The book gives a daily account of the events from the period leading up to his incarceration until his release. The author charges that certain RCMP officers were responsible for his misfortune. His humourous writing style makes this commentary an entertaining read despite the shocking content. This is the kind of story Canadians like to think cannot happen here. A real scandal.

This Troubled nation, J. P. Marchand

This book is a look at Canada's past and future in the light of our current constitutional crisis. The view is that of a Franco-Ontarian who has seen his people suffer injustices that are largely the reason why the French outside Quebec are faced with total assimilation. Marchand writes a controversial history detailing policies that amount to what he calls cultural genocide. He is critical of the unrealistic and costly attempt at bilingualism undertaken by the Trudeau government which he believes only contributed to the fear and contempt that many English Canadians hold of French. Marchand claims the English in Quebec are not a suppressed people, but the best treated minority in the world, and that French Canadians outside Quebec look upon them with envy. Marchand finally suggests what he thinks could be a groundwork for a rebirth of Canada and a reversal of the politics of hate. Some will love him, others will hate him, but every English Canadian should read him.

If you are interested in these or other books, please write or telephone:
Voyageur Book Club 82 Frontenac Street, Hull, Quebec J8X 1Z5
(819) 778-2946
or contact your local book-seller